The Brilliant Socrates and the Foundation of Western Philosophy

Biography Books for Kids 9-12
Children's Biography Books

Western philosophy was formed in part by the Greek philosopher Socrates. He was known to question just about everything and became one of the strangest and most exemplary Greek philosophers. Read further to find out more about this Greek philosopher.

Socrates was born in Athens, Greece on 469 BC and died in Athens, Greece on 399 BC. He married Xanthippe and they had three sons.

While he did not reject the standard Athenian religious beliefs, his views were unconventional. He would often refer to God instead of the gods, and would state that he was guided by a divine voice from within.

HOW DO WE LEARN ABOUT SOCRATES?

He did not write his thoughts down, but preferred to speak to his followers. Two of his students, Xenophon and Plato, wrote about his work. We have learned from Plato's dialogues that indicate he had a major role in discussions about philosophy. Xenophon became a historian and wrote concerning events that occurred during Socrates' life. We also learn about him from plays written by Aristophanes, a Greek playwright.

Anything that was written by Socrates remains non-existent. Because of this, any information regarding his philosophies is dependent upon other sources. A comparison of these sources exposes inconsistencies, which creates concerns about his actual influence. This is known to be the Socratic problem, also referred to as the Socratic question.

In order to know Socrates and his beliefs, we turn primarily to Plato's works, which are felt to be the best source to learn of Socrates' beliefs and his life, and this includes Xenophon. These are known as the Sokratikoi logoi, or also referred to as the Socratic dialogues, which contains documents reporting the conversations involving Socrates.

In trying to learn about his life, difficulty arises in that the ancient resources are dramatic or philosophical texts, separate from Xenophon. There is no forthright history, contemporary with Socrates, which have dealt with his time and place.

Another issue with this is that there is no mention by these sources that claim to be accurate, and often may be partisan. One example would be that the people that prosecuted and then convicted him left no testament.

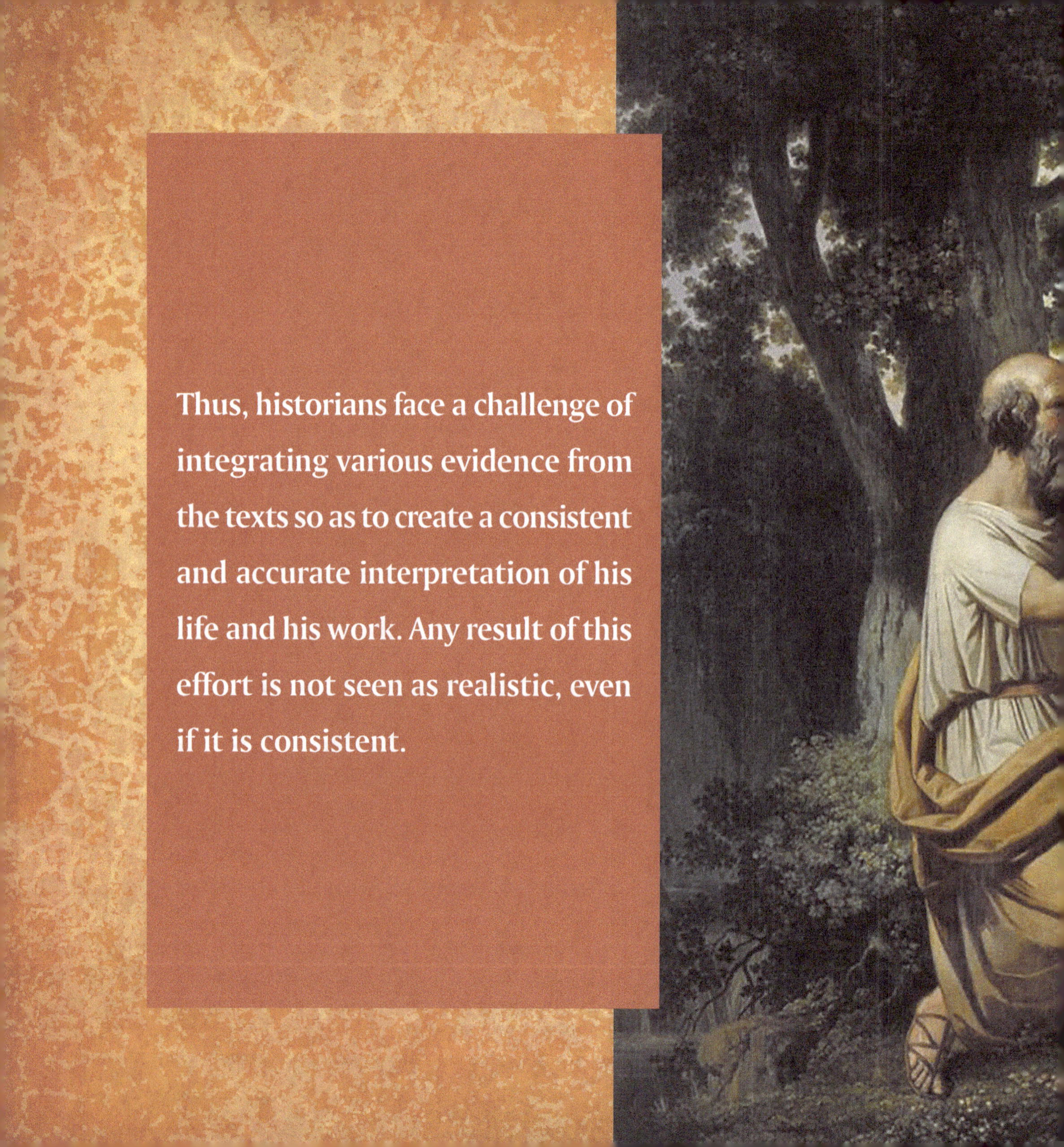

Thus, historians face a challenge of integrating various evidence from the texts so as to create a consistent and accurate interpretation of his life and his work. Any result of this effort is not seen as realistic, even if it is consistent.

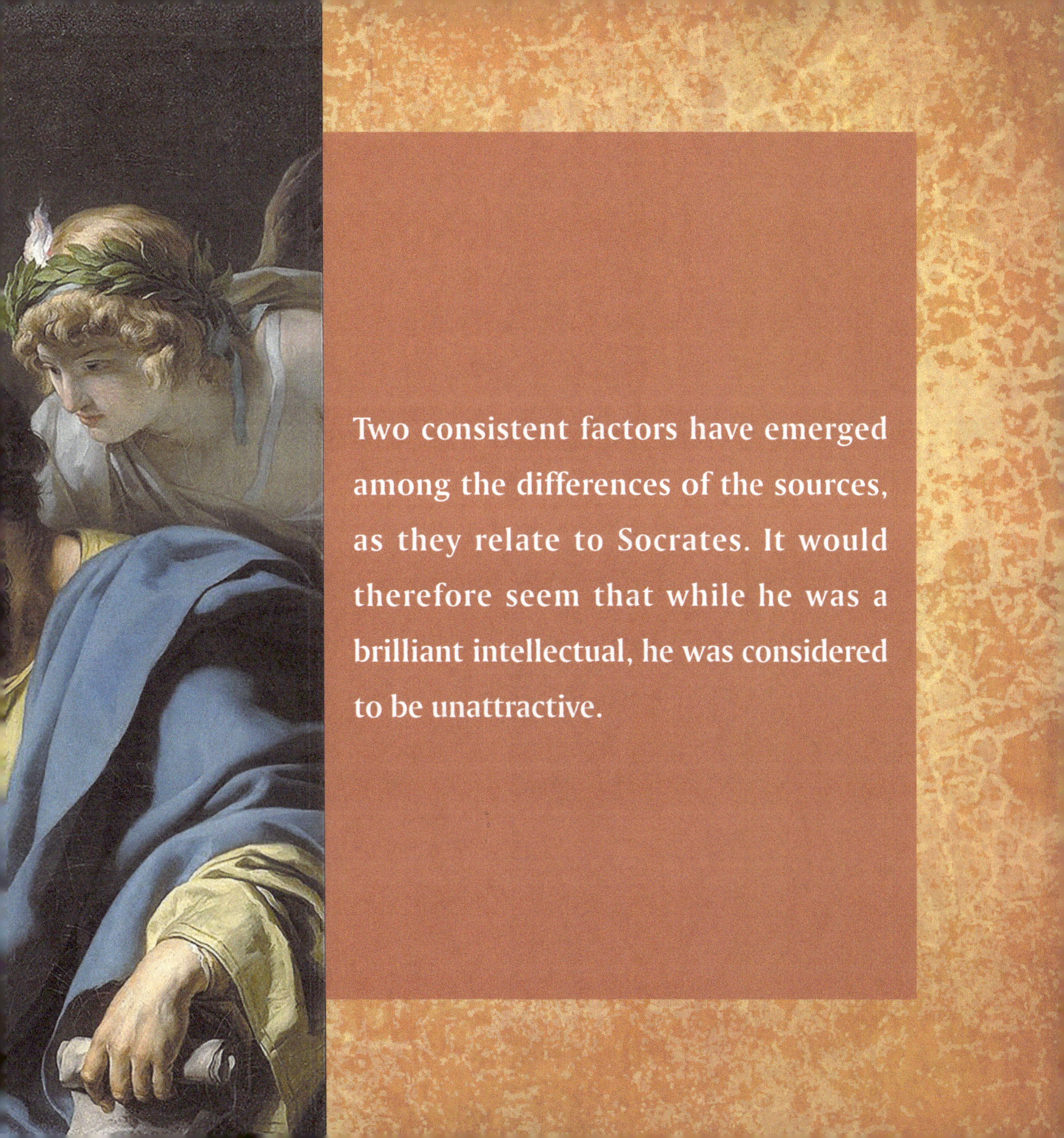

Two consistent factors have emerged among the differences of the sources, as they relate to Socrates. It would therefore seem that while he was a brilliant intellectual, he was considered to be unattractive.

HIS EARLY LIFE

We do not know much about his early life. Sophroniscus was his father who worked as a stonesman and his mother, Phaenarete, worked as a midwife. He most likely did not have any type of formal education because his family did not have much money. He started working with his father as a stonesman early in his career.

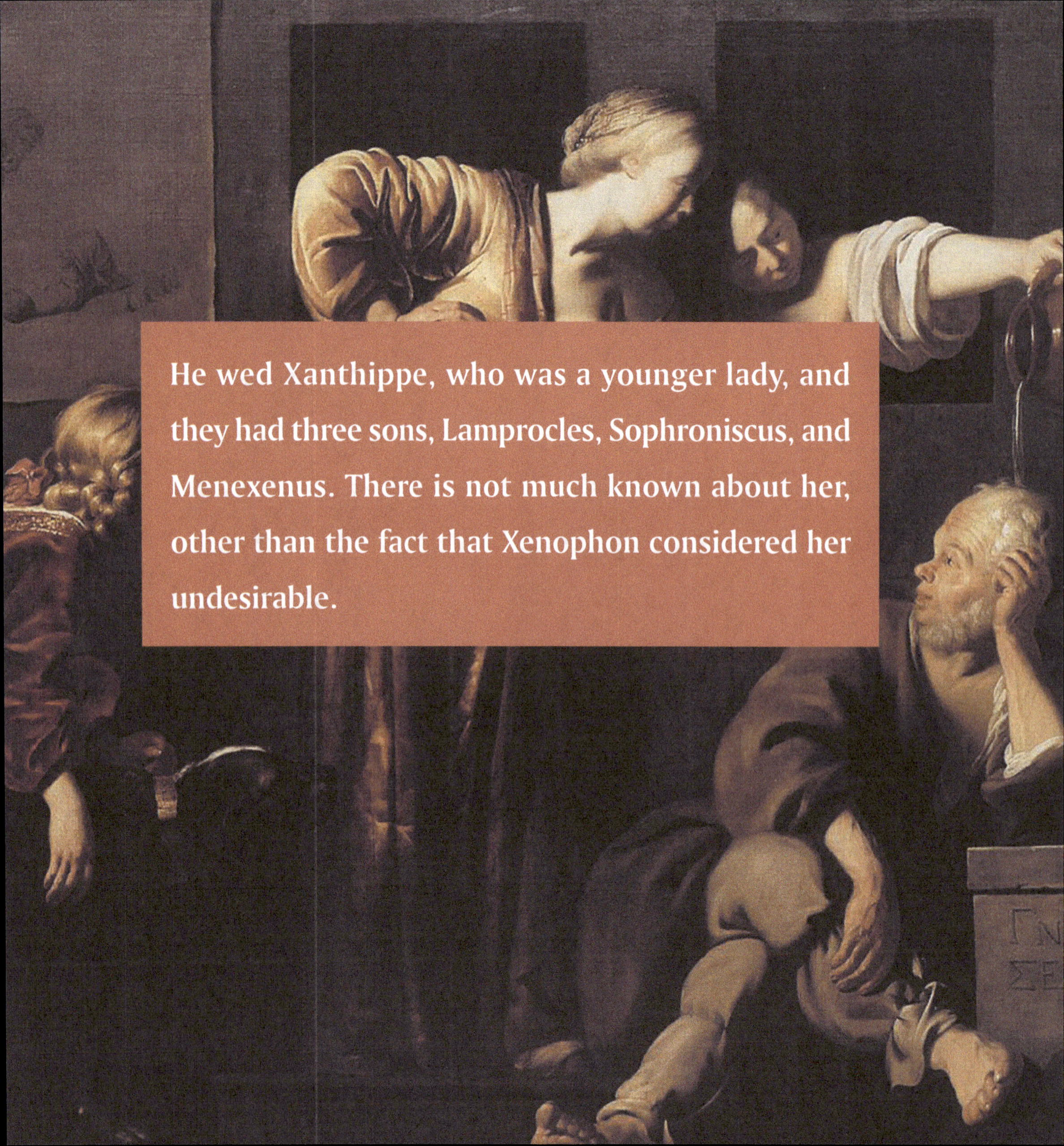

He wed Xanthippe, who was a younger lady, and they had three sons, Lamprocles, Sophroniscus, and Menexenus. There is not much known about her, other than the fact that Xenophon considered her undesirable.

His writings state that he did not like Socrates' second career and felt that he was not able to provide for his family being a philosopher. In his own words, he did not have much to do with raising their sons and was more interested in development of the intellect of the young boys of Athens.

TIMEO
ETIC

When he was young he had a strong appetite to learn. He was described by Plato as wanting to acquire the writings of Anaxagoras, a leading philosopher and he learned rhetoric from Aspasia, who was the mistress of Pericles, an Athenian leader.

LIFE AS A SOLDIER

He lived during the Peloponnesian War. This war was fought between the city-states of Sparta and Athens. Being a male, it was mandatory that he fight during this war. He became a "hoplite" which was a foot soldier. He would fight using a spear and a large shield. Socrates was known for his valor and courage and fought many wars.

TEACHER AND PHILOSOPHER

As he grew older, he started exploring philosophy. He would focus on integrity and how a person behaves, other than the material world. He believed that happiness arose from living a good life, not in material possessions. He would encourage people to practice goodness and justice, not power and wealth. His beliefs were quite extreme for this era.

In Athens, scholars and young men would gather around him for discussions about philosophy. Their discussions would center around ethics as well as any current political issues taking place in Athens. Socrates would choose to not provide answers to these questions, but would instead pose questions and then have discussions regarding possible answers. Other than believe that he knew all answers, he would respond "I know that I know nothing.

He had an exceptional method of exploring and teaching subjects. He would first ask the questions and then respond by discussing the likely answers. These answers would then lead to additional questions and would eventually lead to a better understanding of the topic. This process came to be known as the Socratic Method.

He would avoid any involvement in politics and would count on his friends during the power struggles that followed the Peloponnesian War. He was selected to serve in the assembly in 406 BC. He proceeded to become the only opponent to the unlawful proposition to take some of Athens' generals to trial for not recovering the dead that resulted in the battle against Sparta.

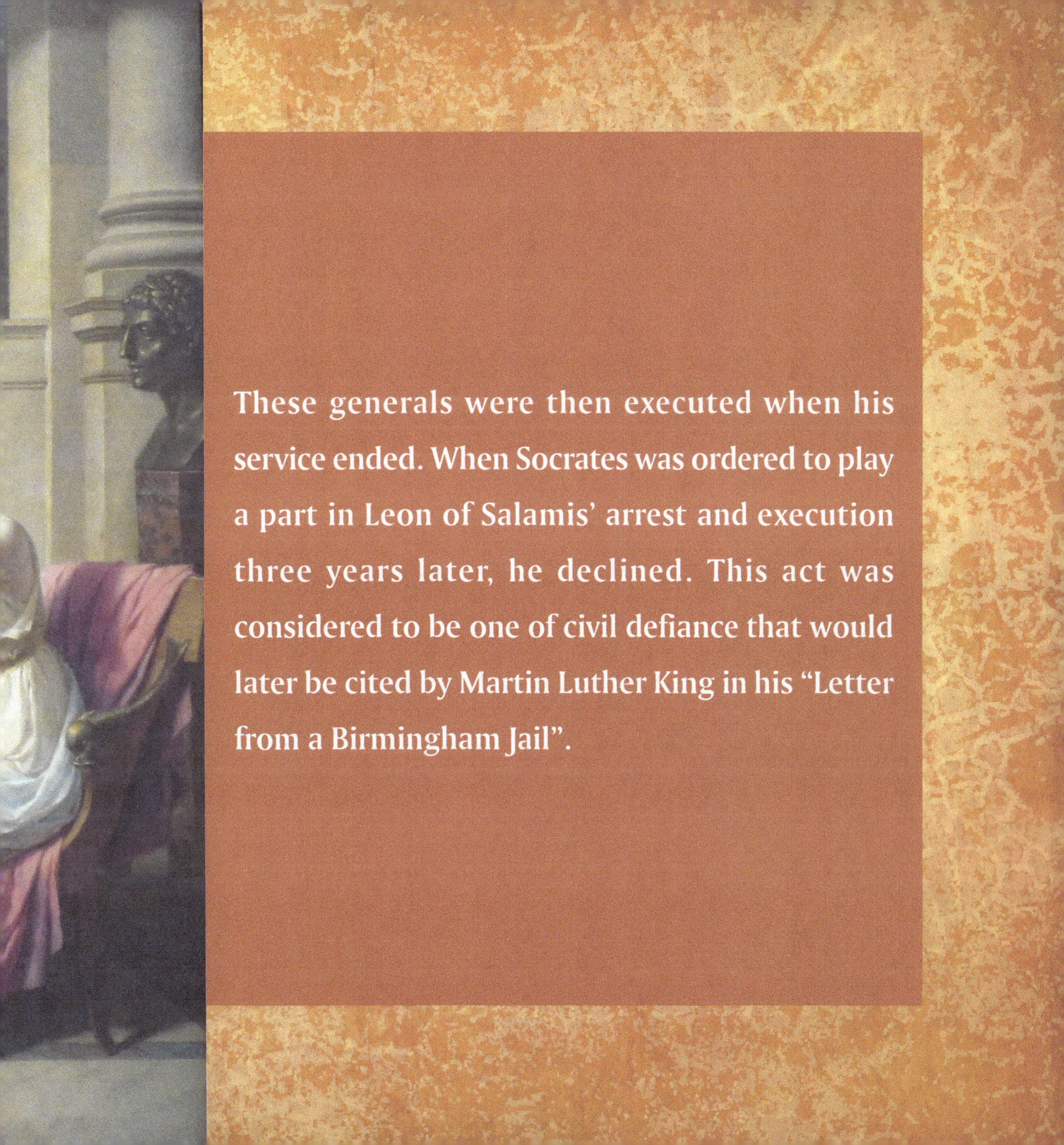

These generals were then executed when his service ended. When Socrates was ordered to play a part in Leon of Salamis' arrest and execution three years later, he declined. This act was considered to be one of civil defiance that would later be cited by Martin Luther King in his "Letter from a Birmingham Jail".

TRIAL AND DEATH

He was prosecuted in 339 for not honoring the Athenian gods and corrupting their young, even though the tyrants had been forced from their power. While many historians believe that there was some type of political conspiracies behind this trial, Socrates was convicted because of his thoughts and teachings. Plato remembers his spirited defense regarding his virtue in front of the jury, and he then he accepted their verdict calmly.

ΕΡΟΣ

During the trial, he suggested that he should be paid a wage by the city rather than being given the death sentence. Because of a religious festival, they delayed his execution for 30 days. During this time, his troubled friends attempted, unsuccessfully, to persuade Socrates to escape. He more than likely could have escaped, but chose instead to face the accusers.

On the 30th day, Plato said that he "appeared both happy in manner and words as he died nobly and without fear". He was given a cup of hemlock and as he drank it as he paced until he could no longer walk and then he laid down, with his friends surrounding him, waiting for the hemlock to kill him. Just before he died, he spoke these words: "Crito, we owe a rooster to Asclepius. Please don't forget to pay the debt".

The Greek god known for curing sickness, Asclepius, and more than likely Socrates' final words meant that death was the cure, and freedom, of one's soul from their body.

In Why Socrates Died: Dispelling the Myths, the author writes about another explanation of his final words. He feels that Socrates was a volunteer scapegoat and that his death was the remedy for the misfortunes of Athens. Taking this view into account, the token of gratitude for Asclepius would signify a remedy for the ailments of Athens.

Lysippe (370-300 avant J.-C.)
Le portraitiste d'Alexandre le Grand
Lysippos (370-300 BC)
Alexander the Great's portraitist
Lisipo (370-300 a. C.)
El retratista de Alejandro Magno
Platon, philosophe grec
Aristote, philosophe grec

LEGACY

Socrates is considered to be one of the forefathers of modern Western philosophy. He influenced Greek philosophers such as Aristotle and Plato. Socrates' philosophies continue to be studied today and the Socratic Method is used in law schools and universities today.

Socrates is also considered as one of a kind among the other great philosophers and he is remembered and portrayed as a religious figure or quasi-saint. Almost all schools of the Roman philosophy wanted to call him their own, with the Epicurians dismissing him, and called him "the Athenian buffoon".

Along with his followers, Socrates expanded his philosophy from attempting to understand this world to attempting to tear apart one's innermost beliefs. He had a love for definitions and questions and this passion inspired development of systematic ethics and a formal logic from the Aristotle era, the Renaissance, and then into the modern era.

His life then became an example of the struggle and importance of life, and dying, in accordance with one's well-examined principles. Benjamin Franklin, in his autobiography, reduced this belief to one line: "Humility: Imitate Jesus and Socrates".

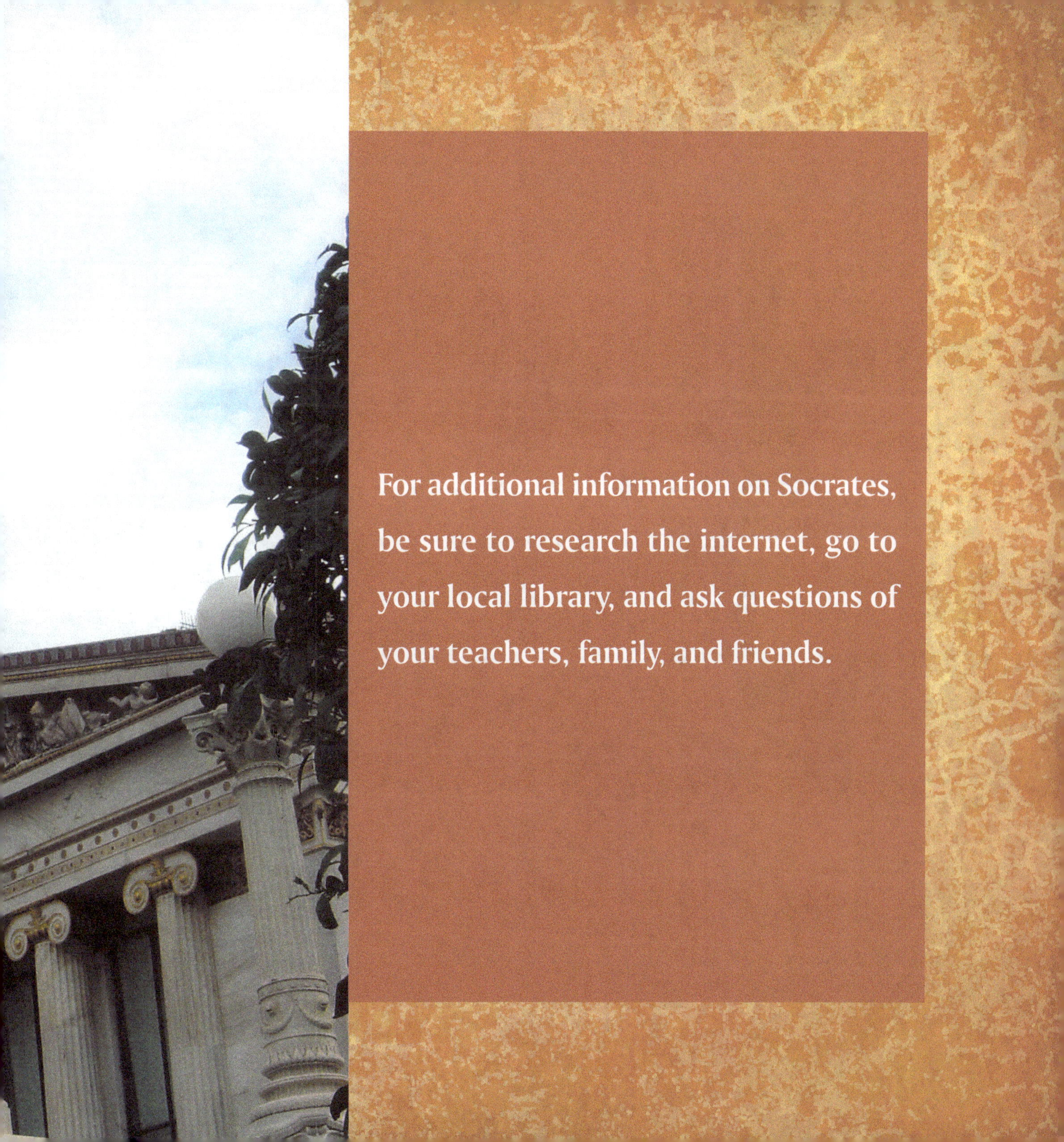

For additional information on Socrates, be sure to research the internet, go to your local library, and ask questions of your teachers, family, and friends.

Visit
BABY PROFESSOR
EDUCATION KIDS
www.BabyProfessorBooks.com
to download Free Baby Professor eBooks
and view our catalog of new and exciting
Children's Books